JULES MANN
KAREN NEWCOMBE
GINI SAVAGE

THANKS TO OUR MANY INSPIRATIONS, ESPECIALLY
ROBERT HASS, BRENDA HILLMAN, GALWAY KINNELL, AND SHARON OLDS.

© 1997
The Norton Coker Press
P.O. BOX 640543
SAN FRANCISCO CA 94164-0543

ISBN 1879457555

DESIGN BY JULES

Table of Contents

Table of Contents

Ginkgo

By the time I get out of the shower
and the young cat gets in to watch
the water run down the curtain,
the street cleaning truck is coming
around the corner and the old cats
bolt for the safe underneath of the bed
as they've done three times a week
for fourteen years, never having divined
that the horrible roaring was not
coming to get them in particular.
And then I might wake my love, or might
reset the alarm depending on the day,
and she might ride with me, gripping
the door handle and flinching all the way
downtown as half-asleep or half-witted or half-mad
drivers weave run red lights change to our lane
without looking or make sudden right turns
from the left-hand lane. Other days she
rides her bike following the packed, late,
diesel-spewing buses down Market Street
towards the campanile of the Ferry Building
and the freighters passing on their way
out of the Golden Gate. These things pass
quietly, and our thoughts rise and leap and
sink like dolphins, so that we do not see
the ginkgo trees on Folsom every morning
while we think "Today I need to call Jim
and get keys made for my brother's visit
and check with the mechanic about a new
clutch and there's the conference call at
eleven . . ." And all the while I'm looking
at the ginkgo trees and ten thousand others
look too every morning as we wait for the green
light and plan our days and our worries.
Four times a year we notice when the trees that

(CONTINUED)

were so green yesterday are all yellow today
with a lowering autumn sun right in your eyes
they shine like Van Gogh's, and again one day
they are startling in their nakedness and rain
on the first heavy day of winter that breaks the
back of the long dry months, and again they become
visible the day they are covered with hard green knobs
that mean the by now tiresome rains are nearly over,
and one suddenly hot late May day when the fog is about
to roll in for the first time you stop planning your day
and just look:

Exposure

My battered hat
at a rakish angle
topped with a plastic rose
Alice in Wonderland on my lap
umbrella staking out claim
to the bit of beach
where I have sat these ten years
I was watching her in the bloom
her back to me—
tousled towhead,
shoulders too broad
when she turned around
unlined face with green eyes,
wide forehead, open as the sun,
breasts and slim belly,
summer's day face.
The dazzling boldness of her look
exposed me to my bones
until I saw that she was me
twenty years ago.

a white dove left hovering alone limb by limb

nervous with lust   nothing happens
the night ends the way it began
on the way to dinner it starts raining away everything
attending to something all the time (constantly)
does not make it work   no more attending to
the need doesn't matter has already been met
or has failed   the material read in the dream
has been forgotten and cannot be retrieved
upon awakening   there are other people in the house
it is dangerous taking what is yours
from somebody else's possession   thoughts don't count
caring doesn't count   opening
things up to look inside is only allowed on
certain days   a large crowd of
people need something   lives are very large

Awakening

You were there all along
hanging from the tree, silent
as I walked past you unseeing, waiting
for me to reach out, to pluck you
and bite into your sweet white flesh,
waiting to be made whole of love
as I waited to be.

Softball Yeats

David pitcher bowler runner goader brother son - man
Grace or Prayer or catch a soul on my shutter for David

He could be my son
if I were browner
with his deep gravel voice
and body beautiful and satisfying
as a child is plump.
It's not puppy fat, he looks edible,
his bones covered in the right places
he's all the witch hoped for Hansel to be
reliable convincing firm and unbowed
he stays close to the ground when he runs
his center of gravity low
this small powerhouse
this veritable engine of passion
he throws out his arms, crucifixion style,
in extravagant gestures to God, as his witness,
looselimbed and graceful,
praying for guidance
he has to touch palms in high fives
when anyone scores, jubilant,
for the softball game he is master of
while he quotes *The Lake Isle of Innisfree*
free and wildly out loud
I want to weep but don't dare to
my shutter jams on his iron calves
I try to catch the poem of his legs
and arm muscles, the sculptured heavy lids
of this son
who is my song

On the Road

1 Away from home

Business travel is ultimately dull, the jet engines
lull me over the clear-cut logging scars,
the skeins of water unraveling 3,000 miles eastward,
the odd runways in the desert, the shiny cluster of silos
in a side canyon. All of it grows between us, a stark land,
sparsely lived on, then swathes of one corn crop
cover several flat states indivisible from the sky.
A freckled hawk looks at us off the right wing,
a two-braided girl is running barrels on
her leggy Appaloosa just before the runway rises
to pick us out of the sky. Hotels smell like smoke,
or have false alarms on winter midnights, or salt
the food to choke you. A business wife at dinner
tells me our founding fathers meant for government
to keep out of the Church, not the other way 'round.
I turn away from her ignorance and think of your keen face,
the line of your hip so like the hills I see
from the fourteenth floor, holy and green,
your voice that could call the wind to your hands,
which hold my distant heart: they are my true home.

2 You traveling

One cat sits in the entry and stares at the door
every moment you're gone, the other curls into a tiny
misery on my lap, a hard knot like the one in me
that can't unravel while mere air is holding you up,
while you are moored in bland hotels.
I wake on your side of the bed, having crawled
towards the smell of your pillow in my sleep.
But you're away and the bed is snarled, the roof
leaks, the sink clogs, hail falls for 15 minutes

(CONTINUED)

from a blackened noon sky. I am askew
without you. Without much to say we stay on
the line a long time, talking up the sweet nonsense
of my dull day and your hectic one,
reluctant to hang up. We do, but I lie awake
half the night, knowing you're flying in the dark
over icy terrain, then wake up to your light voice
calling me from a sleep and a dream I don't remember having,
pulling the covers away from my face to kiss me hello.

First Date

For our first date
I rushed out
and bought black
but couldn't decide
what was sexier
this or that
so I got two
lacy push up bras
and three panties—
that didn't seem
like enough but
I had to stop
trying on because
it was getting late
and I still had
to shower
and get dressed
and drive to your house
with the sexy panties
digging
into my crotch
but I didn't notice

BODY PARTS (sections of an alphabet)

BONES

What light do bones see?
What filters in of gloom and rust
through translucent skin?
Bones long to strip free
the damp girdle of flesh,
jellied organs, the slimy bag of sea
that clings to their armature
like wet kelp clings to skin.
They long to dance a jangling dance,
the bright of bony grace
lacy pure and white.

LIPS

Bitten strip of poor skin, dumb flap,
a flood of red oozes from the snap of pain,
a salty gush fills up the spot,
freshly brightened, smooth and hot
where my teeth bit onto self and set
to take what tiny pleasure they can get.

SKIN

I've grown up enclosing form,
a bag to keep salt water in.
Netted through with nerves,
I'm the lure of all Man's sin.
Dried out by winter cold,
I split lips when you grin.
With age I'll shrink around you,
your youth's shrivelled twin.

Stretched across your raw, live flesh,
I live thin.

Refraction:
Blood from the Orange

I keep thinking about the bottom half of your leg
    despite the fact that your breasts
        were described as your greatest asset

what was I postulating about then
    cupping them in the air
        while you laughed, everyone laughed

I wanted to lean down from the sidewalk
    and kiss your long slightly bent nose
        but I didn't, and you somehow climbed

over the gearshift to get behind
    the steering wheel
        because your door was stuck closed

watching you pull a u-turn across four lanes
    I went back to my room
        that's right: I was bleeding,

I was having a fight
    your voice took away everything
        each separated moment

things seem overturn
    blue sky, blood orange in March
        that fleeting sacramental melt

Sure signs

last week I reached the age

my makeup line stops firmly at my chin
then a rude step down to the jowls below
the neck's pale underbelly

my sketched in artificial brows
thin and sparse
conjure up Cardinal Richelieu
or Elizabeth the First

my inner thighs
fold over
flaccid as an elephant's

saggy rolls
even my quadriceps
need a lift

I pull the skin
back up to cover my knees
draw it up my legs like baggy tights

There.
All safe.
My mental seams straight.

look she said

what are you
if I put my hand
into your gut
what would I
pull out
these are words
on a page
who decides
about the edges
if we were dense
particles
walking around
interacting
that's one thing
but once you start
putting things
out in layers
it starts costing more
I have to talk
you have to talk
so many misunderstandings
when people begin talking
if only we had
one big collective
bad memory
so that only
moment to moment
conversation of flesh
made our existence
illuminate

In Touch

With the Dead

Their mockery is what I cannot bear,
rattling the north window until I come and look
at nothing. There, my name is spoken
in the street's disorder by no one.
The dead shine in details, in leaf veins,
in light's tiny refractions they sing:
I feel their breath on my hair
or hand. People do not seem to care
that the dead flame around them refusing
to be released, touching their fingertips
to our mouths, our salty bodies. Not jealous,
they simply want to finish the interrupted conversation.

With the Unborn

They accuse me of being ambiguous, uninterested
in tiny buzzing voices every time an egg pops
from my bruised ovary. They promise to be scholars,
champions, astronauts, musicians, more poets,
yet they do not arouse either instinct or curiosity
with their velvet pleadings, their pouting carp faces
gasping at the rim of my pond. I know that they
will really become teenagers, drunks, consumers,
so I steer clear of men's burgeoning cocks,
troweled with veins and virility, tune out
the morbid tick of the biological clock,
preferring to keep the clamoring unborn
clearly stuck in the amber of possibility.

With the Living

Why must the living be such a blessed nuisance?
They must hold one in a painful breast-crushing hug,

(CONTINUED)

two beats too long, must put their hands up your dress
or down your pants, must borrow $100 (just until tomorrow)
to pay ... the dentist, must urgently have your
attention as they enter this part of the demonstration,
must offer their advice on your haircut, your mutual fund,
your period, your latest novel *(You poor dear,*
how did you ever get away from that hideous man?
It's fiction. *Of course, you poor thing.)* The living
are a pain, yet I clutch at them with both hands,
pull them close and whisper in their coiled, hot
ears: tell me, tell me.

Death of it

I can feel it tighten inside,
ache as though it were shrinking
the jagged scars of childbirth shortening
along diagonal epesiotomy lines
like a baby scrunching up its eyes against the light.
Would hormones help that opposite
of lustiness, or slippery swelling?
Does a penis shrink in age, like a cunt,
every nick and stitch, notch and conquest
withering, dry as an old leaf—

The crimp and save of dying,
what is it like?
Does it only need
passion to ignite it?
The fire isn't quite out.
I'm becoming less, shriveling
several sizes smaller than the rest of me,
drawn up, cinched in at the neck too tight,
like the waistband of a dirndl,
as if my only real exit and entrance to others
were being sealed.

Do I want blood back
to suffuse tissue?
Is this how the cantankerous bitch is born?
If a man were constantly aware of his prick
dwindling wouldn't he soon be out knifing people
like Jack the Ripper?

Get in the car. Turn the key.
How quietly life burns.

Etch

you laughed as the masks in the hallway turned into our own:
one with a horn in its mouth one wearing a party hat one
sneering with a balloon hanging out of its eye.
you are quite serious as we put them on, one by one, and you
arrange the light and position us in front of your camera
and we become stiff and lean into each other and just as the
last of us gets into place you hear the trigger let go and you
run out of the room to answer the ringing phone because you
heard that your lover was committing suicide and we are
left tilted in uncanny postures laughing out of our monster mouths.

pricksong

which road took me along the shaft
of its ancient tender hard velvety one-eyed muzzle
or muscle? Not a bone in its body
except for a walrus's oosik,
that's a fossil in the first place,
ducks' resemble corkscrews

a shark, all cartilage, is apt to collapse
if the pressure's too great
which takes me to cocks I have known
the ones that bent to the left
or veered to the right, arched and deviated
as bucking garden hoses
and those that swung to and fro
like Himalayan cowbells

the nub-sized virtually invisible ones
blink and you've missed them
the long gaunt lonely ones
too hard and eager for their own good
intent as battering rams
what of the fate
of the men attached to them
puny, casual, lucky, impotent, drunk, underage,
but almost always cocksure little cocksuckers

others, exotic,
shut themselves up in ivory towers
refused to let down their hair
cocked the hoop, or fled the coop,
or kept it up till cockcrow, carousing,
there are just so many
cock and bull stories to be had from those roosters

Come my world-weary
gentils petits cocquelicots,
tender as human beaux

Oh what the fuck!

Ten Years

Dear Bill, yesterday I saw you across the intersection
at Market and Castro
and I thought of that picture you painted
of me with a string of pearls swinging out around my face
I was actually tilted forward but you painted it
as if I were sitting up straight and still
I'm alarmed at how you looked yesterday
lonely and scant
one morning in our kitchen you stood by the stove,
waiting for water to boil, and said you'd noticed
love handles – at twenty-seven you were finally getting
a man's body and I felt sad, too, watching
that delicate hustler body leaving our lives
one of your feet always pointed out, knee bent
fingers tucked in your front jeans pocket
that's how I knew it was you waiting on the corner
I didn't recognize those red
rashes across your David Bowie face
and you didn't recognize
me staring to make sure I wasn't seeing ghosts
you were the first man I knew who wore mascara
and taught me how to put it on
we'd also wear ankle weights to firm up our butts
walk around the house feeling better already
talking about how good it was going to look
real soon

Mirror

Now that I know you are gone
I have to try, like Rauschenberg,
to rub out, line by line,
your picture . . .

                    Mona Van Duyn, *The Creation*

Waiting, listening at the door a moment
each time I left,
to avoid passing you on the stairs—
behind me the cats watch, their eyes disappointed.
Traffic passes outside. A motorcycle.

To meditate, I knelt on the wood, on an old beach towel,
with a candle.
I leapt up once, someone was on the fire escape,
but I could see the neighbor's kitchen right through her.
My reflection. Does loss pare you down so,
like soap, thin and transparent?

I watched myself carefully, passing your door,
to appear confident and detached as a Vogue model,
empowered by your absence. All appearances.

We were polite once, without intimacy,
carefully choosing what each revealed,
what would maintain our cheerful stasis.

Canvases accumulated,
some layered over in cracked impasto,
the wall and floor stained with oil.

We held them up to each other,
like violent dresses—
we waltzed slowly with mouths
nearly touching,
clearing a space on the cold floor.

(CONTINUED)

I slept in your bed,
naked in the curve
where you lie naked.
Alone with your deep pillow
and the smoky, male scent of your skin.
But somewhere between the dance floor
and home —
you slipped off like the glass shoe
and went to try imposters on for size,
while I pulled the heat of the dark blanket around me,
pretending it was you.

Your hands tremble when you touch me,
or when you touch paint,
and when we paint together crouched on the floor
two dark heads inches apart over the paper,
silent,
we have no souls or bodies
swaying across the room from each other,
like dance before a mirror,
emptied and blind in the work—
you have no eyes
I know I have no eyes.

All night, some nights,
I'm up. Downstate, you might be awake.

We could talk about a future.
I want to say — Look, there is none.
Do you think I hardened my heart
out of hope?

I can't ignore or wake you,
or whisper promises. Late, walking the insomnia—

lust will not unclench itself from me.
I run along the hill in brilliant dark, moon air
cold on the drunks who crawled up here to sleep,
scavengers, gulls.

(CONTINUED)

You want to tell me what you learned, that we get old
so I have to work, work
and do not waste time
for there will be no peace.

I want to eat your voice. I want to tell you
how the work shapes your body so that
you will never be free of it.

We must have arrived within a week of each other
two shop workers on the street of tourists and hustlers.
The vendors' stands were heaped with leather cock-rings,
hair gel, poppers. You never said anything, just let me
talk stories and blew smoke in my face.

I had nothing and only wanted a childhood,
or love,
or some work to strain every fine cell
of my body into use.

You were peripheral, waiting for the day
I'd shut up, sit down, hold still.

Spring I was sick in bed
vomiting three days running
while you made love to some man
on the floor outside my bedroom door,
playing the stereo loud enough to keep me awake.
I was feverish enough to think
the strange man in the kitchen was not real,
until the fourth day,
when I got up and made us all pancakes.
I don't remember if that was before or after
I clipped the car on the corner
with the U-Haul full of your stuff that was
too big to get around the corner, but it was
the least I could do.

(CONTINUED)

The truth is I wanted to erase you.
But had no tarnished graphite line to work on,
just your remembered laugh,
last year's foamy chrysanthemum
for a white message —
your body pressed against me in a crowd.
In the air your absence has vacated
I am un-twinned.
A shape and a pure color
begin to stand clear,
enough of myself removed to see you,
apart.

Yet I am the one in your dreams,
dreams you cannot remember or describe.

deserving memory

words take us   it's not that I deserve
   (for after all who deserves anything)
nor   am I entitled   a moving expanse
      nothing makes sense
an expanse of moving emptiness
      morning sickness   at the core of   being
we can't escape from
         as if life were on the tip of
          the tongue
     understanding a stone's throw away
        words torture & bind us
hold us to their hearts   like lovers   once uttered
     they become promises for the future
when or where did I   ever   promise   that
       that was someone else   with another set of feelings
     fool   did you think you had   something to say
         that could be said
       you live   you die   bang   you're dead
    best get used to it   there's no here   after
your life is a Dover Beach more than a Grecian Urn
    and you're my last duchess's husband
      (I won't quote   you should know)
and live by these   if you're depressed   adolescent or both
   confused   alarms   darkling   plain   ignorant
armies   clash   by night   in truth   pain
 but passion   pleasure   fresh in the babe's eye   world
    has neither   wrenched from our mothers
      we run with the ball
founder   revert   complain   attract   deliver the mail   take
    the medicine   in those five seconds
 when the essence of our life comes up
   what will there be to remember

Clang Raven

                              Wing

                              flung
                              black
                              satin
                              gloves
                              skied

                    god's white round spire cap

        my pentagram   of ravens

Cemeterre

Thief, recall this crone
writ in your hand spiral

shotgunned cigar smoke, eyes
faking face, shake the cane

jacketed scapulas
dance, barb my hand's each palm

confessing this: how far
sick with one lean needle

rook croak shaping the dance
teeth skulling his dull kiss

                                              Shadoe
                                        in one scale
                                              sickle

                              moon

rapt
we listen: dark
caw   (CONTINUED)

Dear R,
The year and a day since you, the money and disappeared yourself, flaunting itself on the neighborhood has been five crow, cunning to get the squab from that god's eaves. We dreamed you in so many, but you turned faraway, we called her breath to speak: no reply.

Make us an answer, then
until,
your K

Dear R,
Today hot the hottest day, the silent man staggering with puncture wounds, with a wagging puppy, woman punching her mastiff which took her right arm and gave one shake away. One. She white-faced shivering, screaming "Get Get away Stop looking at me!" Do you remember?

a coward your K

Dear R,
We do speak of you.

in balance,
your K

Dear R,
I asked the moon about you, when I stood in her shadow. The soft surface was close and warm, a breath on the back of my hand. Though she'd been low enough to smell of wild rosemary from the hills, she had not seen you

up that hill,
your K

Dear R,
Did *not* go to die? Who leaves wild weed at the door? Broken tooth here on a string? A curse on the stairs, say nothing: the wind, a grief, a lost friend to come in. Will have food, when you come home. Little to say but singing.

a left yet,
your K

C l a n g   C l a n g   C l a n g   C l a n g   C l a n g

Snailaway

'A gastropod doesn't wear its head or heart on its sleeve,
but its stomach on its foot, hence the Latin name.' V.S.

Night-furtive snails lurking underleaf,
skulk for safety, cower under terracotta.
Late layabout snails posing as pansies,
Madame Récamier snails reclining,
gourmet gastropods nestle on beds of lettuce,
wilting or plain arugula
romaine endive chicory.
I pick through the booby-trapped salad,
a gourmand's beaten me to that last honest leaf.

They make snail sushi, so I'm told,
Snail *Alfredo*, *Escargots Rossini*,
snails with *pêches à la mode*
coq-au-vin, or *vol-au-vent*ed,
(legion on my aquilegia)
omeleted snails *al burro*,
pests *al pesto* unconfined.

Mesquite herbals, snails *al fresco*,
Wellington-style baked in batter,
snails whipped to mousse
soufflées, abricots Chantilly,
snails *flambées* or
Tex-Mexed prairie snails
slouching in desuetude.

Extra-pizza-topping snails
chicken-fried and jumbo-roasted
tiger-striped or tiger-balmed,
Occidental accidentally
trodden on, on purpose
dopey snails tripped out on acid
Acid snails slamdunked in vinegar

(CONTINUED)

Thousand Island dressed
for their overnight cotillion

Red snails in the sunset
Pale in the moonlight, covered in dew.
Maggoty snails to start the barbeque
Snails jerky, snack and trailmix,
leaf-laying babies in jellied clusters.

'Shall I compare thee'.... to a slug
Thou art more rubbery than temperate.
Earthquakes may strike the Hayward fault
but all spring snails should now be ground to bait.

'O to be'....
in a snail-free state
now that April's here! Debriefed,
deroofed, dehoused, dank and sexy,
dark and drunken in my Anchor Steam ....
slip your way past me to oblivion!

Tomato Soup

It came out lumpy.
What a waste of milk;
I won't eat it.
It gets colder and thicker.
It became warmer and thinner
when I heated it up:
      out of the can
      and into the pan.
It has a wrinkly, bumped skin
all over the spoon, the bowl,
its soupy self.

When I was a child,
I crushed saltines in and slopped it up
against the winter.
Now, grown,
I take it with pepper:
for pain.

Whether to go to Pisa

You call early and as you begin talking I
keep getting this mental image of the
eyes of a woman in the park today as she
looked at me, sun-friendly skin heavy-
lidded eyes for once in my life I thought
I could wake up to those eyes and I tell
you how I tried to nonchalantly get a
glimpse of her body when she bent down
to pick up the ball—and you tell me what
it's like to know everything about some-
one and have to hide your attraction
because you are the doctor they are the
patient—I look at my wood dresser and
it reminds me of her hair the rich dark
swirls of it and how it looked different
this morning as she walked towards me
in the park, bigger, less tamed, and how
it feels like our bodies lean too far
forward, too familiar as if we've been
there before, there's no control of a body
never having known a body knowing
where to pause, where to hover, which
way to look—and then you explain yet
another impossible relationship and how
all your crushes must be leading up to
something big—and after we hang up I
have this flash of getting off the train in
Siena, all the buildings were cast in a
bittersweet shade with vivid tufts of
green there must have been some smell
in the air close to what I'm cooking
tonight they say aroma is the key to
remembering everything.

Inherence

Women are unlikable.
Riddled through with
their mothers' merdey essences,
they cry:
"I am NOT a marble cake!
Angel!
I am angel-food!"

Pick pick pick with the
undersized soul forks.

Chocolate crumbs.　　　　Blonde crumbs.

Two crumby piles.

Hanging together for a story

After SNAKE by D.H. Lawrence

Two headless rattlesnakes were brought to me today.
Thick muscled fangless cords,
nerves not yet dead,
writhing yellow-black patterned marvels,
alabaster rattles rustling like corn.

I put a twist-it round their tails
and hung them up by the base of their rattles
on the humming bird feeder hook
where they oozed their life down
one silent drop at a time,
continuously swaying slow whiplashes,
dancing to an inner music.
I draped them over the arm of a deckchair like stoles;
they kept falling off and sidewinding away
on their bellies.

Their lack of eyes and fangs removed the fear
not the fascination.
They were so strong, slow, energetic;
they wore their diamond markings
with such dry elegance.

Unable to part with them
I carried them around in a plastic Safeway bag.
My friend, their killer,
thought I would want to slit them
along the pale length of their soft bellies
with a carpet knife
and peg out their skins for hatbands.

I couldn't while they still moved.
But I didn't want them to be wasted
and they began to smell faintly.

They began to smell more than faintly
as I opened the Coleman's cooler
where they lay in state on ice,
rigor mortis setting in.
I wanted to keep them forever
like those dead pets of childhood,
couldn't bear to think of them
deprived of life so I could walk safe
and barefoot among the vines.

I did not want to see your colors fade
wanted to feel your life continue
to muscle into each curve
responding to my curious fingers,
fierce energy meeting energy,
would gladly have reattached
your narrow heads to your slack long bodies.

In life so heavy
in death so light
where did the ounces go?

I always believed
snakes do not wish to be killed;
that if I could rattle a tail
and give my enemies a sporting chance to escape
the venom I carry.
I would consider that enough warning.
I would not wish to be killed,
driven out with expressions of disgust,
for my mere existence.

Pleinaire

pampas and cypress

seed pods of something lifting above the tangled clover and wild strawberry
(auburn leaves this time of year, low to the ground)

several toadstools grey as a dead tooth on translucent stalks

something that looks like (but doesn't smell like) sage

entire hillsides of iceplant tips shaped like a child's drawing of fire

dabs of pink flowers, and white, in the midst
of the flame and yellow tint where mid-morning shafts of sun
meet the groundcloud remnant fog

raccoon tracks risk across the sand

Sharon dances

Isadora Duncan
in an egret's body
gives herself to the dance
swoops dives   glides
shakes her legs
her pauses as crucial in movement
as they are dramatic in speech
her arms raised in unselfconscious praise
free floating but she does not take
her sandals off on grass she
finds the earth too cold
mating rites of rare
dark skinny bird
in a wood clearing
transported

Thinking it is Dawn: Because the Moon is so Bright the Birds Start Singing

Walking into moments: Yellow dashes of Orioles
Light from a swollen stream: Orange flower (full of Monarch Butterfly)
Impatience giving way: One lavender Shooting Star
This slowly getting to know you: Juniper tree without berries

Everything that isn't here yet: Leopard Lilies Miners Lettuce Rosehips
Arriving in Sheep Valley: Seven audible rushes of water
All that is immediately seen: Lupine Marsh Mallow Paintbrush Larkspur
Monkeyflower Cow Lily Forget Me Nots: Phlox Columbine Salsify Primrose

Deciding this: In the middle of things
Sly beat of mothering quail: And not giving in
The bent foreleg of a deer: Worn through one more winter
Feeling how softly the fur remains

Three Quarks for Muster Mark or How Can There Be So Many Elementary Particles

(after reading *The Quark and the Jaguar* by Murray Gell-Mann)

It's some comfort to a poet to learn
that the quark (or "kwork" as Mr. Gell-Mann
would have it said) is first found in (guess where?)
Finnegan's Wake, Joyce, as per usual,
being ahead of himself and us had
anticipated this fine foundation
of physics, this most primary motion
flickering in God's eye, really the most
elementary of the particles.

Comfort becomes concern when we learn that
singular quark is now available
in eighteen varieties: three colors
and six flavors. How to tell what flavor
you've got with only three colors? Some would
put back the tart ones after they taste them,
making the whole business more sticky.

To further complicate (surprise surprise!)
poor quark shares its elementariness
with antiquark, electron, photon, sweet
twins muon and tauon, boson, poor odd
higgson, and least but not last, the wily
neutrino, blithely passing from the sun
right through the Earth, behavior Updike called,
rightly, crass.

Add these to their anti-kin, the total
reaches sixty, no, that straggler higgson,
sixty-one. Sixty-one? Madness! What sort
of primary any-damn-thing is that?
Adding insult to injury, Gell-Mann
tells us elementary particles
are possibly infinite in number

(CONTINUED)

and largely invisible to us. Well,
they're all invisible, and what he means . . .

Damned Hell if I know what he really means!
Now orchids, that's another thing, only
a few odd millions of them, vanilla
flavored, visible to the naked eye,
requiring no knowledge of the New Math:
phalænopsis, paphelopædilum,
oncidium, cattleya, lælia,
cymbidium, miltonia, calanthe,
brassia . . .

Notes from Tahiti

peter is watching a crab sidle along the ground. a coconut falls from a tree and lands on top of the crab. the scuba divers go out to feed the sharks. they get out of the boat and line up in a solid wall of bodies. the people on the boat throw food into the water directly in front of the divers. the sharks come. they eat the food and do nothing to the divers because their eyesight is so poor they think the solid formation of bodies is a wall. every morning the tide comes into our bungalows. two beds at high tide, standing there in six inches of water. I wake up and go over to the edge of the room where our knapsack and shoes and guitar are, and I begin putting things up on the table. it nags at me that I don't remember keeping all these things up off the floor before. gina's guitar, especially. then gina wakes up and asks me what I'm doing. now I see two pictures at once, the one with water in our room and the one of high tide down at the beach, and I have to choose upon which to base my actions. I answer that I was just looking for something, and climb back into bed.

Be dirty

Not enough time for it, laundry in particular, oh and the dryers never worked so the clothes grew in nests on the floor, then shifted to a basket. The basket moved to the hall.

A moment came when there was no clean underwear, but fishing in the basket yielded a pair not too far gone to be worn inside out.

The day after that it was socks. Dishes congealed in the kitchen; who needed to wash more than one a day to eat on?

The thought occurred to her that it was a waste of time to sit in the kitchen with the lights on every night. So she turned them off. Sometimes she sat in the dark living room, looking at the patterns of passing headlights outside.

No reason for bathing, after all, who cared? How mortal. She developed a smell, intimate as bread; musky—not quite the sharp, pissed-on smell of the homeless, but a disturbing animal scent.

The bed had a beigeness of sheets, but she hardly slept, for she was turning into something else and restlessness was on her as she waited in the dark.

When she went out for food, the neighbors asked if she were okay; she saw them in the hall, confused and tiny, at the far end of the binoculars, scurrying. Her movements were deliberate and planned with care.

Night after night she ate macaroni and cheese. Once she bought eggs but dropped the carton in the hall and stood watching the yolks spread, scum over and begin to dry.

For the duration

history stopped
as she popped the umbilical into her mouth,
ceased dreaming the past,
born today, fully clothed, hair permed,
equipped with court shoes,
enough food and a flashlight to last her,
husbands' and wives' thefts irrelevant,
lovers, all that muddled insomniac yearning,
had happened to someone else eons ago
and those abortions, well they were just babies,
babies

Cleaner

New varieties always appear. He is in the store the day they are delivered reciting the properties of the new chemicals.   The hardware stores save him the best European brushes, the finest cotton rags. He lines them up in his pantry, each in a bin or on a nail.

To get at the cracked corner under the bathtub he wears a biker's headlamp. He coaxes out every grain and hair that fell since 1904 with a stiff toothbrush. Finally, as he takes out the double-bagged trash, he is free of that history.

When he first began the cleaning, he found a tiny metal diver under there, dropped and forgotten during a child's bubble bath.

The stiff brightness of his shirts endears him to his neighbors.

Nob Hill Cocktails

after the valet parking
a cliché of cymbidiums

in the marbled halls
unavoidable white and malachite rooms
& flowers so huge they almost topple out
of their own arrangements
onto their flat faces from ming vases
proteas and stargazer lilies
poise on columns of black jockeys

the man allows women to arrange him
like repertory curtains coming down

Cassatts & Renoirs jostle on the walls
lit by tiny halogen spots
the women in swathed silks
and smooth stretched faces
gnarled hands aglint with icy diamonds
greet each other without eye contact

they descend in droves of beaks and sequins
a black flurry of Van Gogh's crows

sharp pointed noses & uncreased lids
no jowls or dewlaps
but plumped up collagen cushions stuck
above their cheekbones
like Chaucer's furies
they take their place unchallenged in society

smothered by their zealous claws and wingtips
he is still, soaking up their love

(CONTINUED)

when they speak they pay attention only
to the inner solipsistic voice
guiding their words and acts
they smile as the camera directs
smiles that don't quite reach the eyes

                    he tolerates their ministrations
                    as would a mummy in an iron lung

about to crack, they never wear thin
glazed as eggshells on fresh-faced eggs
they toss their coiffed too-perfect locks
coquettishly
as far as the taut skin allows
in local Gazettes
they appear having a good time
in Cancun or Malibu
they smile and smile again
in Cozumel, their craggy John Wayne counterparts
weathered by alimonies, parasail

                    why he can barely breathe for their stuffing
                    their curiosity makes him choke

with bejeweled hands now like bacalhãu
there are no flies on their canapés
no books but massive coffee tables
with Meissens of lemons, canaries and parrots
no waste paper baskets
no cat hairs on their cashmere
or camel hair smoking-jackets

                    is it they who prey on him
                    or he who is the predatory victim

                    unreasonably loved with his silk grey eyes
                    crêpe de Chine longing & siren's gift for song?

The non-event

When I'd been married seven years, my husband's oldest
friend, Jerome, hirsute and deep-voiced, stroked my thigh.
Confusing sex with love, I asked a friend for the key
to her apartment. Only Jerome was so shit-scared he grew
impotent whenever we tried fucking—He was married too
and not used to unleashing such passions in people. My
predecessor was a tv reporter with places to go like
Washington D.C. so didn't really mind if Jerome was all
goods and no delivery, but I'd been waiting earnestly for
passion all my life. Each meeting required weeks of care-
ful planning, babysitters, warning my friend to be out.
I'm glad now that we never made it because, come to think
of it, Jerome was a bit of a bore. I cut his wife's face
out of the photo he gave me.

slice

We're the first people there and it's one of those bohemian San Francisco
wrenched out of the Mission district because an aunt died and left an
empty flat in North Beach kind of party. Desdemona is my date—I only met
her last week but I like her name so I'm pursuing her. This is some long-lost
friend of her's party and she told me she won't know anyone here so we're
even. The guests begin arriving in a stream that pushes us further and
further towards the back of the livingroom. I've finished my first beer and
have to go have a cigarette on the front step. I emerge back inside into a
solid mass of bodies and immediately jam up against a gorgeous neckline I
suddenly recognize as one I'd been staring at just yesterday at Cafe Flore
where I had a table indoors with a good perspective on the tables outdoors
right on the other side of a pane of glass. This view had inspired me to grab
a napkin and start composing a lurid encounter with the creature this neck
belonged to when my elbow got jostled by a drag queen dressed as
Madonna and we got into some queeny conversation which caused me to
lose my other train of writing thought. Then when I left the cafe this hot
body on a black 1953 Motoguzzi barely tamed her beast into a parking spot
on the sidewalk as I stood there and stared at both of them. One hell of a
day in the old neighborhood I thought as I stumbled across the street in a
daze only making it as far as the median before the light changed,
stranding me on a desert island with this goddess Ursula I used to follow
around on Castro Street surreptitiously store to store and hadn't seen in
years; I stood basking in her beauty until the light got green again. So.
Meanwhile I'm jammed up against this neckline at this party and actually
don't mind but finally we disengage and I am surging back toward
Desdemona. I'm just about to gently nudge a tall brown leather jacket out
of my way when she turns inquiringly and I almost fall dead on my feet it's
her again the goddess Ursula at this party right where I am and I feel like a
toad because I know she doesn't recognize me even after all those years on
the same street—she'd never looked right at me like she is now. I duck
between her and the person she's talking to and run right into that drag
queen Madonna only since Madonna didn't bump me I bumped her I don't try

(CONTINUED)

to jog her memory about our encounter yesterday I just get up on tiptoe to try to locate Desdemona. She is very far across the sea of heads. There is nothing left to do but drop down on all fours and crawl through the remainder of the room guided by the unwavering planks of hardwood floor. I wouldn't have minded that someone just stepped on my fingers making my right hand go limp except that it's Desdemona in the act of cruising Ursula who did it and that really makes her drop a few notches in my book after all I'd done for her by accompanying her to this party the least she could do is show a little more sensitivity about my existence. It's like in the short time I'd been away she'd forgotten all about me. This really makes me mad and we get in this big fight only we can't stomp out—we both have to get down on all fours to leave. This time I just put my head down and try to be as inconspicuous as possible though it isn't easy especially when I run up against an intimidating wall of motorcycle footwear but I don't look up I want to know but I don't want to know. Back outside we sit on the front doorstep panting and of course I see the '53 Motoguzzi parked up against a tree and now I'm sitting in my bathroom alone again practicing my french reading the warning label of the wall heater and wondering how they could condense a beautifully composed paragraph of instructions *en français* into simply "do not operate without legs attached."

Shame

the guilt producing
hot flash inducing
thoughts
like the time
I was thirty five
and hid in the closet
when your dad walked in
in the middle of our fucking
it was the kind of closet
only the English
perhaps the French
still have
poky, Welsh
with an oval mirror
and a mean catch
and I had to step up inside it
flatten myself back
into the adolescent smell
of armpits, sneakers, cigarettes
stale jeans
it would not have done
to have been discovered there
in the bedroom
of his sixteen year old son
though it was fun at the time
exciting too
you were no longer
a virgin and I didn't think
I was hurting you

My father, the engineer, the fly fisherman

*Weeks into the run, there are people taking in the paintings one
by one, and you can tell from the way that they're moving close,
studying the surfaces inch by inch, that many of them are artists.*
JED PERL ON ART

As I catch up to him in the Corot
collection he's leaning forward,
I lean with him
to where he points
at the delicate shoots
of undergrowth
behind the cottonwood
each leaf
formed entirely with dabs of dark
green and light, the way it feels
when you put your hand
into the branches
the way the leaves
interplay
with the rippling stream.
"And look right there
past the cottonwood,"
he says, "that's
where you'd catch one;
see the way the rock stops
the water—that's
the perfect pool."
And he draws his hand back
from the dappled branches
and stands
perfectly still, near the water's edge,
his body leaning forward
knowing how hidden it is
just a shadow
behind lightness of leaves.

Storytime

With one pink roller in my fine infant hair
to match your grown-up rollered head,
we sit in the kitchen of 1959,
waiting for Dad and the babysitter.
While you try to decide what to wear, I eat
macaroni & cheese. Miss Agnes comes first,
smelling of vinegar in her lavender, flower print dress.
You tell her I can have one scoop of ice cream,
take my favourite stuffed duck to bed.
Then Dad gets home from work and you're off,
a dream in your pale, embroidered dress.
Miss Agnes has green spots in her sugary hair
where her parakeets creep about on their blue feet.
I lie awake, or think I do, but pretend to sleep when
the headlight beam brings you home. Miss Agnes goes.
You wake me for a midnight fairy tale:
                              The Emperor's New Clothes.

My heart is slow and trusting

for my father

My heart is slow and trusting.
It sits like a deaf mute on a wooden fence
watching the training of horses.
I try to protect it from the final kick
at its full, unfastened place.
It comes wrapped and tied at the neck
like Rigoletto's Gilda in a sack.

Yet I still find listening to the ascending
and descending scales of Don Giovanni
sends shivers up my back,
and recognize my love of music
came from you
who used to conduct me on your knee
as if I were Beethoven's 9th,
took me to see Faust at the Met
when I was four and
explained the whole story patiently
so I could understand.

You galloped me round in a glory
with your beaky pregnant skittering
half-run half-walk,
high on your shoulders.
You quickly tired when we were alone
though I was your willing hungry toy.

Once you took me to a fair,
bought me a leaf-shaped nacreous pin
with my name *Virginia* in cursive
copper wire, I thought was gold.

No longer the pretty child,
now you wouldn't recognize me for flesh.

Not for flesh.

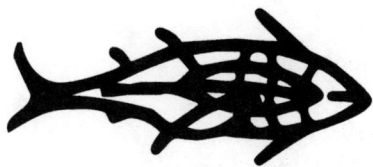

The Garden

i.
The gate to the garden is not hidden.
That sound of rustling satin just behind you
is not a pigeon seeking sparse greens
from the sidewalk cracks but the bright angel

who prevents us each entry. The shaft of heat
on your winter blanched arm is not sun's radiation
but the flaming sword that beats us out of Eden,
out of Avalon, every day. The gate to the garden is here

where the street is split open by a buried brook
and mud sluices up during tremors,
within the storm drain's lost mosses
or across the fennel-choked empty lots.

The scorched apple trees in the yards
of neglected rental housing units
are the lost orchards, the loose dogs turning
out trash are the wise wolves of Eden, the tabby

in the window is God's lioness made small,
diminished by the choice to bide with us,
as we daily diminish ourselves.
The angel beats about you like the memory

of a dead lover. The garden gate is closed.
Past the tarnished coins, rusted knives,
broken bowls, orange surveyor's staves,
is the hidden door. You could go through.

Beat that whirring guardian back,
twist the day and open the gate of blessing.

(CONTINUED)

ii.
You can feel it when you lie on her body,
locked into her, that her heart,
deep within her, encloses a dark forest,
that deep inside the trees, past finding,
lies a cleared grove, green with light,
and a ring of standing stones within it
surrounds a well, where the breath between
the syllables of your name lives,
and the ladder that drops into the well,
inside the most unreachable
darkness of your lover's heart,
is the door to the green world,
with only your skin, and all of life,
to keep you from entering.

Poetry on the Yacht

reading eileen
myles just
then a swarm
of light
silver-blue fish
occupied the green
water below me
in the
morning before
the sun
got too
high & turned
everything blue

in the middle of john ashbery   a storm breaks lasts five minutes
          his words patter and clip
                         under the awning then hang in the air
afterwards condensing
          everything that moves

william carlos williams at sunset

Hitching

Me and Marcie are hitching in New Mexico when this guy in a pickup stops. We know it's not safe, we weren't born yesterday. I had another friend who got raped, held up by her own Swiss Army, the kind with tweezers and doodah for getting stones out of a horse's hoof. So anyway this wall-eyed guy with pigtails offers us a ride to Taos (I'm a D.H. Lawrence nut). He makes Marcie sit in back where the dog's tied up, he says there's too much junk for us both to sit up in front, but I know he wants me 'cos I'm the blonde. Says he has to stop at his rancho, check on the horses first (Marcie's big brother taught her judo and I know some moves so we figure okay).

Well the guy starts chugging beer, passing a joint, feeling up my thigh, things like that, and I don't like the smell of his breath or the look in his eye. He has a rifle and knife on the dash. No fucking penknife either.

When he stops in a remote spot under a tree, walks round the back for a rope and starts 'hoo-hoo'-ing for the horses to come like some weird owl, me and Marcie don't bother to wait. We start off real fast towards the road, praying.

He calls after us 'Hey girly girls I didn't mean to scare ya, two pretty little schoolteachers like you. Here you come back here now, I thought all you white girls liked kissing.'

Kiss? My ass.

Wild Dog

He cannot speak.
He tries to wind
that earnest tongue
around a word,
as though to have a word
were to have a soul.

Were he a man
he would still thrust
his long cold nose
between your legs
to know who you are now,
who you will become.

If you became
like him you would
toss off your human shroud.

If you became
like him you would
outrun your spoken name.

The Uttered Complexity of a Symphony

for Ed Mycue

because of the hurrying clouds
the bell-toned toads ringing
each pond along the road
the pensive fields
their knobby-kneed vines
rising up through still water
as white-throated egrets come again and again
to sip the wet gown
as white-throated egrets come again and again
rising up through still water
their knobby-kneed vines
the pensive fields
each pond along the road
the bell-toned toads ringing
because of the hurrying clouds

This is the best time to play golf: late afternoon, shadows

across the greens peaceful as a river pool
with a soft hum of bugs skipping along the surface...
on the days we played a town where
there wasn't a high school girls' team
I'd step up to plunge my tee into the grass
and the boys from the other team in my foursome
would get a look on their face a cross
between panic and disgust
as if I held a secret in that small white ball
about penetrating this privacy of the male spirit

I didn't like to talk at all when I played
it was just a long rhythm of bending the ball
to the ground and swinging
walking up to where it stopped rolling to see
what tilt of grass I was up against
and then choosing a club from among my best friends
and swinging again
towards that pale green pool with its flag beckoning
the lips of grass changed into fine gossamer fringe
so smooth I wanted to get down and
lay my face against it but instead
ran my hand over to check
for moisture and cowlicks and anything deceptive
bringing the ball into the cup
becomes the effect of a guide string
tied between your depth perception
and the truths and lies between the ball
and the hole and the way you finally
move your body shows how loyal it is to your mind.

Victim

The fear of predators is not so much
in that they find our meat a rare delight
but that some tiger, wolf or crow will spite
man's laws, find some hermetic way to clutch
within itself a changeling soul, walk upright
and shed its skin, to go about in much
the way you go, and learn to speak with such
cunning that perhaps in broad daylight

it walks onto your land, into your very
home, proves you dull and stupid, thick and slow,
steals your lover with its glowing eye,
debauches her with skill in your best bed,
then turns you out to wander in the snow
telling how the beast stole hearth and wife and bread.

A Different When

One single sheet of 8-1/2 x 11 paper blew by around 2 a.m. end over end through the parking lot, I watched it as I'd watched for glimpses of your red hair throughout the party, your silky body standing next to clumps of talking people. I wanted to know what it said, on the piece of paper. If I ran after it as it transversed your head-lights, and brought it back to you in the car, would we be able to glean some message out of it—about us, of course, since we were intersecting just then—the law of catalyzing theories. Decided to leave it blank. Maybe it was an angel of blank-ness. Of having nothing to say but go forward, no past scribbling its way through our life, throwing itself in cartwheels in front of us. Go forth, said this permissive blank buddha, leave no footprints from your past—your cozy front seat is not of this world, you belong to no one, whatever gets wet will grow. That enormous clank of a huge ship leaving the dock where we sat, motor running, travelling into a big night with no moon but a square white sirius of blank animism moving in the dark, licking everything around the edges. Where we sat, getting touched straight through to almost nowhere else to go, our words slowly scribbling across the page, the click of a car door opening and closing and the unmuffled contralto of your car departing, the seriousness of silence and how your red keeps drawing near then accelerates in glimpses, compelling me end over end, not blank, anything but blank, into the night, and towards.

Thanksgiving 1994

You're up to twenty weekly shots, three
each day, Sunday two. One a clinic trip
from which you bring me purloined
plumeria you snapped off while the
hospital guard flipped a coin,
pretended he was interested in the distance.

Epogen, you tell me, hurts in injection,
or is it the vitamin complex shot,
or the hormone mix? One of them
builds hemoglobin, another energy.
The new drug fights your personal colony
of microsporidium and suddenly

you've an appetite, gain twenty pounds,
become crabby and petulant — meaning
energetic — you load up a turkey plate
cranberry and gravy you can't finish,
complain about our driving, the cold,
the sloppy ending of a Hollywood film.

We smile when you're not looking
pleased that you want to fight with
everything, but everything, in sight.

The lack

It's in the unguarded watch
when your ear scapes the bone
dead dead for his footfall
velvet tread along back or belly
you wake to the stone
of your mate's dropped hand
mistaken for his svelte body
or his soft thud landing
as he enters the narrow gap
between cold wall and sliding door
that it hits, he's gone for good.
You had counted on his warmth
magic squint, quizzical nose
small reassuring necessariness
the kneading restlessness
before you rolled over and conceded
his rightful place
in the gully between bodies.

We Are All Walking On Water

for Gina

I don't know why I felt the need
to bring pictures
why this sudden
need to share
these flat faces
from my life
with my mother
it's like we all get desperate sometimes
and change direction
as if after being away
for a long time we can assume
the construction has finished
and we can drive straight through
no detours
no walking on water
now that I'm familiar with boat life
I automatically keep an eye out
for moorings
as I cross the bridge
above the Pacific Ocean
two men and one
of their mothers out walking
why do I always assume
they're gay and probably one
has AIDS or else
the mother wouldn't be there
we are all
writing Myles poems
Emily writes one from her roof
in New York and sends
it to San Francisco
we pass them around
to our friends
wondering if we'll eventually reach

(CONTINUED)

those brilliant conclusions
or else go places
past the logic
I can't believe
my mother wanted the picture
Emily took of me after swimming
naked together
now the same photograph
hangs on their wall
I wonder if this
relationship they share
is anything like the lover
whose mother isn't
on the bridge
because he's not
the one

Out like a light

their small deaths parade before us
like children's sparklers
flare for an instant
before going out
no see 'ems, mosquitos and moths
fizzle and splutter on the grid
of the neon zapper, indigo flashes
in rapid unimportant succession
like staccato machine-gun fire
or Gatling's gutteral stutter

we, impervious
on the patio
chow down on spareribs
doggedly chew our barbeque
with chanterelles
swilled down with gamay beaujolais
ratatouille, black walnuts, shitake

we tip back our chairs
to their massacre
chew chops and devilled eggs
to the crackle of their departing souls
are they attracted to the jolt
as we to love?

does God preside in similar unconcern
getting the buzz at a giant computer
loaded with Atlas-sized boulders
munching popcorn and red hot jerky
reading the Godly Times
before She idly leans across to press
our <u>SMITE</u> button?

Kúhhá-ye Zágros

(The mountain range between Iraq and Turkey)

MONDAY
The edge of my desk crumbles
into gravel ridges, recedes in dust
from the corner of my left eye.
I am typing in my blue ergonomic chair.
A woman sits at the edge of my desk
in the dirt.
Her hair limp under her damp scarf.
If I could see her
well enough there would be snow
in the hollows beneath her eyes.
Her eyes follow my hands as I type
a proposal to build a new school,
as I check my lipstick in a tiny mirror,
holding it so as to block her out,
out of sight,
to eclipse the line of people
on the cold road below her.

TUESDAY
The woman is gone.
Scruffy hills still cling to
the edge of my desk, pulling
my attention away
from the insufficient words.
I cannot bring one face
into focus through the haze
of benday dots.
So many move in the long
twisting queue.
The sound of my computer keys tapping
is blurred. A man's tinny voice
pleads with official personnel,
the voice in someone else's
walkman. I glance over—

(CONTINUED)

has she come back?
A hand protrudes from behind the rocks.
Typing Section Three
words spring up on the screen,
golden words made of light.
The proposal will go out
next day delivery.
In vision's periphery
the hand is still,
Delicate.

WEDNESDAY
My hands seem distant.
They come to work
with pretty rings on.
They type automatically
while I am encompassed
in hollow noises,
laments in foreign voices.
Professional lips move as I am given
instructions, but I'm not here.
I peel the back off the plastic
Federal Express pouch,
smooth it efficiently
across the parcel.
In the elevator the crowded
sound is deafening.

THURSDAY
Ballooning far off, radiant parachutes
catch the light. The buildings shake.
Jets buzz the city.
They are outside my window,
down the hall,
away into the mountains.
A woman is crushed by a relief package.
It is as though I had reached across my desk
put my thumb on her.

(CONTINUED)

The pilots are dropping good wool blankets,
helpful bread, boxed water, lightbulbs
and shovels. They wave to the people below.

FRIDAY
Fridays we back up the computers,
slip one disk in the drive at each prompt.
Someone sits on the corner of the desk,
between me and my tiny hillside.
We are practicing for a formal presentation.
The frenzy surrounding a bread truck
distracts me. The men are going away,
going back to fight.
I want to go fight.
The presentation drones on.
A pink face moves with no
sound coming out, body stands,
gestures, sits back
in the inadequate pebbles.
The pattern of the slide show
melts into the shifting colors
behind: stooping women
pile up cairns over the dead.

wondering what sort of day it is before calling

she's hanging laundry out back
my cousin calls her in to talk
she describes bowel movements
marvels at the body
how it works and then suddenly doesn't
surprising everyone
more when it does

and there is too much time
time fills up like another room
ready to go into
I don't know how long to keep talking
I'm afraid something's going to change
or go slightly ajar

and I can't escape it
the voice fresh on the edge
the face that has come apart knowing that everything small
is so present tense
it takes a long impossible reach to clarify things
to know there are two conversations
going on
one in this short language of words
and another that is groping
wildly for something
to hang onto

the day my mother died
Tuesday May 23rd

I hung up on my brother in disgust
for telling me in the same breath
how he had shopped around for a funeral home
two thirds the price of one
the doctor, Doña Alicia, had recommended
and when he told me the coffin
had to be sealed within 48 hours
and I had no choice or say in the matter
when I knew you could lie in state
letting your systems wind down
as long as you liked
in the comfort and privacy of your own home
having a wake with those who loved you
who could minister
and perform the Bardo rites
and ceremonies to prepare you
for your inevitable return to the wheel

Did he want you rushed and bundled
into the ground and out of his life for good
to pay you back for all the phone calls and the pain

On the day you died
I went to the Monet exhibition
twenty two last paintings at Giverny
we had seen at the Marmottan 35 years ago
and withstood the crowds
of diminutive white-haired women
and annoying bulky old men their arms akimbo
six foot tall at least who spread themselves
in front of the irises and lilypads
with pride and satisfaction
pleased to be a nuisance

(CONTINUED)

And the woman on the bench
beside me said her sister sight-impaired
could out Monet Monet any day

And wept for you in the crowd
sorely missed your not being able to see
the colors of the paintings
or vibrant certain brush strokes—
angry and sure talent
his cataracted cataclysmic sight
as bad as yours

You could out Monet Monet
or out Medusa any other Mother any day
your blades sharp as whistles

In Swans, I ate the oyster
savored the shrimp
winced at your absence
watched the swollen back
of the turtle's neck
on the rock outside the de Young
its red cheek stripe glowing
its mumpish parotid glands
swollen from behind when it turned its head
passers by thought him a plastic toy
unreal as a circus painted terrapin

And while you were growing cold
it felt unreal to be there
in front of the giant Buddha
in the Japanese teagarden
that people had thrown pennies into
the lap of so disrespectfully

And searching for Dorje's compassionate
Tulku smile in the Tibet shop
familiar as a touchstone
(Come off it Karma Moffett)

(CONTINUED)

I listened to the bowls and bells
I blurted out why I was there
to the stand-in Karmic man, a complete stranger,
decked out in turquoise power jewelry
a tinker, a tibetan commercial salesman,
trafficker of Buddhist relics,
in amethysts, the spiritual materialist
with his Persian Khatmandu wall hangings
& tingshas (bells)
& photographs of his paintings
swirls that looked like cosmic assholes
& because I had thought Dorje would be there
as he had always been, I told him of your death
my concerns about visions of your still warm
body being rushed away without any Rites
still furious at my brother
whom the day before I had said 'Fuck you' to
for being so pigheaded brutal & callous
even knowing it to be his damaged self that spoke
caused by your early abandonment

And felt so proud of you
for managing to do it, unassisted,
before we had to commit you
or take you back to England,
which you loathed, kicking and screaming
and crazy or tranquilized
(like a wild animal anaesthetised by darts
so they could collect their witless
intrusive data

So proud

And you died alone, stoic in your own home
kept your dignity
with Piri Piri sitting on your chest
probably miaowing for food up to the end
(spoilt greedy cat)
and I knew you to be in a different realm

(CONTINUED)

when I called Monday night
and you'd been able to put the phone up to your ear and say
'Ah ah ah ah ah'
and you said 'Ah' when I said
I loved you 'Ah' 'Mama I love you' 'Ah'
and we had a conversation like this
perhaps for five minutes
or was it ten when all
you replied was 'Ah' at the end of each sentence
I made the sounds aloud, tuning in
to your heart & you told me
I have given up from a deeper place
you weren't in the same distress or agony
& later in the Target parking lot in Terra Linda
your voice loud & clear & fratchety in my head
'Ginpin, I'm doing all I can to go'
as if I had chided or accused you
of overstaying your welcome, resented you
for still being around
it was so clear
the tetchy tone of your voice
& your dead friends & mine
appeared to comfort

and the particular rake
of the gulls at Kronkite
sloping their slow rhythm
overhead & the first pelicans
swooped & pierced their prey
and turned their heads to look at me mid-flight
and you were with me on the beach
even if your carcass lay in a coffin being sealed
elsewhere on the outskirts of a small white
previously unspoilt touristy fishing town—
Portimão or Lagos—
with only a market one sardine factory
& a railway station

GINI SAVAGE, KAREN NEWCOMBE and JULES MANN discovered each other while living in the same house during the summer of 1990 Squaw Valley Community of Writers. That week together—of talking about poetry, breathing poetry, dreaming poetry and stretching personal boundaries of writing poetry—cemented their connection. Since that time they have come together time and time again to share their work, to run the annual Squaw Valley Community of Writers Benefit Poetry Reading in San Francisco, and most of all to challenge and inspire each other to push out and try fresh, new things. GINI SAVAGE worked with the legendary writer Jean Rhys as amanuensis and collaborated with her on her last collection of short stories *Sleep it off Lady* and autobiographical pieces *Smile, Please*. In the Seventies she founded and edited a small gay literary magazine in England that Christopher Isherwood called the best of its kind on both sides of the Atlantic. She was the first person to interview David Hockney and Quentin Crisp on their homosexuality, when the latter was living in complete obscurity. KAREN NEWCOMBE is a San Francisco poet who has been published in *The Paris Review, Carbuncle, Transfer, Gryphon* and *The Squaw Review* (which she has also edited). JULES MANN has work anthologized in: *Zenith of Desire* (Crown Publications '96), *Between the Cracks* (Daedalus Press '97), and *Queer Dog* (Cleis Press '97). A featured reader in the *Jejune* International Poetry Series in Prague in 1997, her poetry will be published in Czech translation in early '98.

THE TRIAD

TRIAD POETS MAILING ADDRESS C/O JULES MANN P.O. BOX 14624 SAN FRANCISCO CA 94114

PUBLICATION CREDITS

Awakening: *Asspants*
A white dove left hovering alone limb by limb: *Minotaur*
Be Dirty: *Asspants*
Etch: *Asspants*
Exposure: *Backspace*
For the duration: *Asspants*
Hanging together for a story: *Asspants*
Look she said: *Loud Nipples* (chapbook, Chi Chi Press, 1993)
Mirror: *Asspants*
My father, the engineer, the fly fisherman: *modern words*
My heart is slow and trusting: *Asspants*
On the Road: *Asspants*
Refraction: Blood from the Orange: *Minotaur*
Slice: *Minotaur*
Ten Years: *modern words*
Thanksgiving: *Asspants*
The day my mother died: *Squaw Review* (Chi Chi Press, 1997)
The Lack: *Asspants*
The non-event: *Kumquat Meringue*
Three Quarks for Muster Mark...:
    Squaw Review (Chi Chi Press, 1994)
Victim: *Asspants*
We Are All Walking On Water: *Backspace*
Whether to go to Pisa: *Asspants*

COLOPHON

This book was created in Pagemaker 6.0, on our sacred Macintosh Centris 610. Title font is FFErikrighthand and FFJustlefthand, designed by Erik van Blokland for Fontshop; text font is Trebuchet; back cover blurb is set in Minion BoldOSF. The "running women" cover graphic is a depiction of a petroglyph of women running at Oenpelli, Unbalania, Northern Australia, donated by Michael Barry of Australia. The petroglyphs appearing inside the book are from a shareware font "Cave Painting Dingbats" created by Michelle Dixon. Cover stock paper is from the Wasau Celebration Series.

Printed by Four Seasons Printing
in San Jose, California.

BOOK DESIGN BY JULES